Mom,

T5-AFT-507

"The purpose of life
is not to be happy -
but to matter, to
be productive, to be
useful, to have it
make a difference that
you lived at all."

Our world is a happier
place because you're in
it -
         Happy Birthday
              Love,
              Mark o
               Sandy
              1977

Touched by
The
Master

Touched by The Master

Reflections on My Life and Mission

By Audrey McDaniel

Floral designs by Hazel Hoffman

The C. R. Gibson Company, Norwalk, Connecticut

Copyright © MCMLXXV by
The C. R. Gibson Company, Norwalk, Connecticut
All rights reserved
Printed in the United States of America
Library of Congress Catalog Card Number: 74-83777
ISBN: 0-8378-1770-6

Contents

AUTHOR'S PREFACE

This book is written with a prayer that it will reach the multitudes and that I may share with them the way my life was changed when I was . . . *touched by the Master!*

Let me preface everything in this publication by saying that I shall stand forever in awesome wonder at the miraculous way in which God works His wonders in human lives through His Son, the matchless Jesus, and the beautiful Holy Spirit.

All credit in my life and my work belongs to God, for He has been the . . . talent . . . the divine agent in extending this work of love. The mission belongs to Him alone.

Indeed, God opened a window of heaven and poured out His blessings upon me as this story of His love unfolded in my life.

I shall try to relate this blessed experience exactly as it happened to me. For I think this is the way Jesus meant His ministry to be — a love of simple truths — uncomplex — not the impossible dream but the reachable star. For His is one love for mankind.

These words from a well-known hymn best express my sentiments: "I love to tell the story because I know it's true . . . It satisfies my longings as nothing else can do."

This miracle of love that happened in my life goes back to my childhood for its beginning.

God in my Life

AS A CHILD ...

My father died at an early age and my mother had to go to work to help support us. She, my little sister Dorothy, and I lived with her parents — my grandmother and grandfather.

My grandfather was such a great person in my life. Although he was a busy executive, he was so much fun, quite a humble man, and always so interested in me and my sister. Granddad was Supervisor of Telegraph and Telephone at the Washington Terminal, better known as Union Station, in Washington, D.C.

Gram was as good as gold to us in a practical way, but not too outwardly affectionate. This was always of concern to me. Fears seemed to dominate her aging philosophy and I wondered if she had had a strict childhood or just what it was that made her so rigid in her discipline of Dorothy and me.

By contrast, my mother was extremely affectionate, sentimental, and kind. In fact, she was more like a pal to us, always calling us darling and treating others in the same endearing manner.

Mom worked at an investment banking firm as a telegrapher. She had learned her trade of "working" a telegraph wire to New York in my grandfather's office at Union Station. It was a very unusual occupation for a woman in those days.

My mother would sacrifice to buy my little sister and me dainty dresses. She loved big taffeta hair bows for my naturally curly hair; she always dressed me in pink and bought blue things for my sister. I was brunette and Dot was blond.

Mom seemed instinctively to understand all the special things associated with childhood and bought us the prettiest dolls and carriages — even though sometimes I knew she could ill afford them. Christmas was always extra special to her.

I remember one Christmas season Mom had the dolls and carriages delivered ahead of the holiday to a friend's house so that this friend could make beautiful accessories for the carriages — which were as large as real baby carriages.

Then on Christmas Eve, a snowy blizzardy night, she and my grandfather went to this friend's house to get the dolls and carriages to set beside the Christmas tree. But on the way home, a stranger, seeing my mother and grandfather pushing life-sized carriages in the snow storm that dark night, commented: "That woman must be crazy to have those babies out on a night like this!"

Next morning, the dolls in lace and ruffles with ribbon trim on their dresses and pillows and coverlets also lace-trimmed — one in pink for me and one in blue for Dot — were sitting in front of the Christmas tree. My grandfather, who always went down first on Christmas morning, was standing in front of the carriages. So were my grandmother, my mother, and my aunt to hide them until we got there. Then they all stepped aside and smiled at the surprise on our faces at discovering such lovely gifts from Santa.

I loved to have Mom read fairy tales to me and I adored

flowers. In later years she told me that as a tiny girl I would always say to her that I had to have a "pretty paley" — meaning flower — and she said my heart would break if we passed one and I could not have it.

In those childhood years, I was a chubby little girl with brown eyes and long brown curls. I was also, my mother told me in later years, a quiet, serious child. I remained chubby until I was about six and then, when I fell victim to years of illness, I grew frail and thin.

When I was about eight years old, my mother became critically ill. I remember my aunt saying, "We will put a little necklace of mine on her that she has always loved." One day Mom appeared to be dying and I remember sitting in a chair almost numb with fright, tightly gripping its rungs and praying every single moment that God would let my mother live. I kept telling Him over and over that a little girl as frail and young as I just had to have her mother.

God understood that little girl's anxious prayer and answered it. In time, my mother fully recovered her health and lived to be eighty-four years of age.

But most important of all, that prayer to heal my mother brought God into my life.

As young and insecure as I was, I understood that He was my help in time of need. He had proved to me in that answered prayer that He was my own dear heavenly Father and a loyal and true friend.

From that time on, God was my constant companion and this was the bond of love that would some day take me to the fulfilling climax of this story . . . this story of God's infinite love.

All I could think of after this was His friendship. In my

child's way of thinking, my heart simply knew that *His help had made Him mine.* Just as I accepted my mother in the faith of a little girl so now I accepted God.

In later life I realized that God had turned those anxious hours of my mother's illness into a divine plan.

Before Mom's illness and her desperate need of God's help, I had heard her speak of God. My grandmother would also speak of God and her church and how she was a charter member of it and sometimes helped prepare the communion wine. So I had heard something about God — but now His loving, precious help in time of great need had brought Him *for real* into my life. Here was truly a Father who cared for me and all of my childish needs — and my heart was satisfied.

Thus it was God's love for me, and His help, that brought the love out in me for others. Surely I give to Him all credit for it.

This, then, was my very first religious experience — *meeting God,* not just hearing about Him. It was to be much later in life that I would come to know Jesus as well.

Meeting God in this way had helped me forget much of the pain of the past. I refer to the time when I was six and had had to undergo neck surgery some seven times. The wound did not heal until my tonsils were removed and my recovery took about a year in all.

Even when I became very ill again at age eight, things did not seem as bad as they might have — for I knew God was there. This illness was at first thought to be pneumonia but was later diagnosed as rheumatic fever.

I drew strength from knowing that my wonderful God had healed my mother. And there she was during this par-

ticular illness of mine patiently reading my beloved fairy tales to me. She was such fun, living every experience with me as if she were my own age.

I also lovingly remember the day during that sickness when a package arrived from my Sunday school teacher. It was a box of chocolates. I recall how I crept out of bed as Mom went to answer the door. I wanted so badly to look down from the upstairs hall, but when I got out of bed I was so weak I fell. In the weeks ahead, my temperature rose each day until the illness grew to quite serious proportions. But gradually, with God's help, I grew stronger and finally recovered my health.

That illness when I was eight caused me to miss a whole half year of school. When I was well enough to return to third grade, the teachers wanted to promote me on trial just the same, for my grades in the past warranted this. But my mother insisted that I start school again exactly where I had left off. She assured me that it was no disgrace to be half a year behind my classmates since I had not been there to get the work.

Mom turned out to be right for this helped me to learn the missed studies under much less strain. From then on, I started getting top grades in every subject — and kept on getting them right up to the eighth grade when I graduated as valedictorian of my class.

Despite this academic success, I never felt very smart in school. I seriously felt the need to study hard and I always needed God to help me do it. During these school years, too, I often felt God all around me, for my teachers were all so kind to me.

13

Mom had warned me that the seventh grade had seemed a bit harder for her and that it had been quite a transition period in her own school days. In so warning me, she was preparing me for anything unpleasant that might come — she was always so protective and understanding. But, as things turned out, seventh grade proved to be great, too, and it was packed with love.

I will always fondly remember my seventh grade English teacher who always wanted me to recite *Evangeline* and other poetry from the front of the room. I constantly wondered why she asked me to read so often for her — but how she would praise me for it!

Little did I dream way back then that God was continually weaving a plan in my life and that someday my mission would be speaking out for God over the air waves.

A few years earlier, when I was ten, my mother decided to remarry. I remember her coming to us one night from her honeymoon to tell us it had been decided that we — my sister and I — would remain with our grandparents, who could not stand to give us up. This arrangement would allow Mom to adjust to her new wifely duties.

I did not want to hurt the feelings of my beloved grandparents. Yet when I heard this news I began to cry. I remember hugging Mom around the skirt of her dress and saying, "Mom, please don't leave us behind!" Mom just quietly comforted me and promised faithfully to come back often to visit us.

Poor thing! I remember thinking in later years, she was entitled to a new life and love of her own. Of course she'd been torn between hurting her parents who had helped her

so in time of need and hurting her own children. Yet I am sure she made the right choice in the end.

I look back on it all now with no sadness or regrets, for in those lonely moments it was just another reason to look to God for my help.

At any rate, in the years that followed my mother would visit us a couple of times a week from the office and have dinner with us at Gram's. She also took us places and bought us lovely things; it was always such happiness to look forward to seeing her. We came to call it Mother's Night when she would be there with us.

I remember on one of my birthdays at Gram's Mom putting a gold locket in an empty Limoge china vegetable dish and placing the lid on it. When I came to dinner I just thought I was being served a vegetable, but when I took the lid off, there was that beautiful locket and chain. Even in those days, when Mom wasn't always under the same roof with me, God was putting happiness in my life.

I recall on another birthday I received a very special gift. It was Robert Louis Stevenson's *A Child's Garden of Verses*. The highlight of that day was when — perhaps because I'd had too many cookies and ice cream — I had to go to my room before the party was over. There I read for the first time that marvelous poem called "The Lamplighter."

To me, it was so wonderful to think of Robert Louis Stevenson who, though very ill, still had the courage to build a lovely and imaginative world of his own among the folds of the counterpane on his sickbed. After all, I'd been a shut-in myself and I knew.

Curiously perhaps, those inspiring lines in "The Lamp-

lighter" always meant this to me: *O Larry, I'll go round at night and light the lamps with you!* For in my heart I felt that I actually met Larry the Lamplighter each evening at dusk. With his little stick he would stand at the end of the walk of each home and light each lamp. Truly, I felt that I walked to the door of each house with him and, in so doing, left the spirit of God to help those souls inside as God had helped me.

I could scarcely know then that someday, in my own way, I myself would be composing inspirational verse. I would one day write these words:

> *Dusk with soft shadows falling*
> *At the quiet close of day*
> *Moments of meditation*
> *When I turn to God to pray*
> *There in the evening of silence*
> *I ask my father above*
> *Please hear my earnest pleading*
> *Watch o'er thy people with love*
> *Strengthen their faith, dear Father*
> *Bless them each step of the way*
> *Then grant them peace in sleep, Lord*
> *Thy sweet Amen of the day.*

By the miracle of God, these same words would later become the script for my radio and TV sign-off. I would be narrating them to beautiful music in the background of the studio.

Indeed, when I little dreamed of it in those early years,

God was doing the spade work in my life for a later, greater service to Him.

My teen years were a series of ups and downs — mostly downs. When I was fourteen, for example, a heart specialist discovered I had a weak heart. In the weeks that followed, infusions of calcium, transfusions, and other kinds of special care were necessary for I had serious anemia as well.

By this time, I had graduated from the eighth grade and entered high school. How well I remember marching with my classmates from the old grade school to the brand new high school. As we paraded, there was my grandfather sitting on a park bench waiting to wave to me as I passed by. I had warned him not to call me "little sweetheart" in front of the other kids for I felt quite grown up at that point in my life.

Then suddenly, just a few weeks after entering high school, the heart specialist advised my mother to take me out of school lest a more serious heart condition develop. So I was largely self-taught in the years that followed. I even learned to type at home.

Although my teens were full of shut-in days, they were also years packed with sacred and inspirational meaning. I was at an impressionable age and, in addition to my heart specialist caring for me, a new and wonderful family physician entered my life.

This doctor, who was the son of a Lutheran minister, became an ideal figure in my life. He was so kind, so tender to the ill. Once I saw him arrange a job for a poor, frail man just to make him feel useful.

Often he took me with him as he made his afternoon calls to see his patients. I would read a book as I sat waiting

for him. Before we came home, he would usually buy me a big glass of milk or an ice cream.

This fine doctor became an inspiration in my life and strongly influenced me to look up to life's finer things. His guidance caused me to know that in all kinds of ways God was teaching me the way of His Love.

I cannot emphasize too strongly the role this dedicated doctor and friend played in my spiritual development. To this day I feel that God put him in my life to help shape my goals and aspirations.

I remember how he would come to my hospital room from his office way across town late at night to bring me some special food because I ate so little. He had already checked me during the day but would return at night to feed me. Always very concerned about my health, he would tuck a napkin under my chin and say, "Now, Chickie," — which he had nicknamed me — "tell me all the things of the day."

Then this considerate man, knowing how cooped up I had been in the hospital, finally let me go on a little vacation when I was better. At the Casa Loma Hotel in Braddock Heights, Maryland, the sunshine and fresh air did improve my condition. One day I looked out the hotel entrance and his car was parked in front. He had brought a prominent bone specialist from Johns Hopkins University along for the ride. Both men were laughing and they had brought along with them a sort of net with a long handle. Presently they told me this was a butterfly net and they were going to teach me how to use it. I am certain my doctor friend had come to check up on me — but I didn't worry about that because we had so much fun that day chasing butterflies.

I remember, too, how he let me go and stay with some dear friends in Cumberland, hoping again in his great heart that such a trip would make me feel I was making progress toward recovery. But when I stayed a little too long to suit him, he called me long distance and chided, "Chickie, you come right home to me."

All these experiences combined to teach me that our life's participation in God's plan must be tempered by kindness, thoughtfulness, and concern for others in the fullest sense. This is truly the sweet way of God!

My dear doctor friend loved me in this generous way until he died. I will always remember the love expressed for him when he went home to God. I had never seen it done before, but bouquets were placed on each side of the walkway to his gravesite and, after the interment, someone seeing me standing close by lovingly took a yellow rose from the big casket bouquet and handed it to me. I brought this flower home and put it in a tiny hand-painted vase and to this day that vase brings back lovely memories. It still inspires in me that happy glow in knowing the perfection of God and the way He has the power to create guardian angels on the highway of life.

Through all of this recovery period in my teens, my beloved grandfather played a major role in my life. Forever ringing in my heart will be his words: "Little sweetheart, better days are coming." Little did I dream how prophetic these words would one day prove to be.

As my health steadily improved, I felt the need of doing something more active. I told my grandfather that I wanted to teach a Sunday school class at a nearby church and asked him if he could arrange it. He said he would try.

Now my grandfather was a devout Catholic, my grandmother a charter member of a Protestant church, and I myself was aspiring to teach in another Protestant church. Our differing religious directions had the effect of making me feel that God's love knew no particular faith or creed . . . only love for all mankind.

My grandfather did intercede for me at the nearby church and soon I was given a small Sunday school class to teach there. One little girl in the class felt she could not attend regularly because she did not have a sufficient variety of clothes to wear. The thing that concerned me about this was that she might miss the opportunity to know the wonderful Friend I had in God. So I made some little dresses for her out of my grandfather's old shirts, adding pieces of other material to complete the garments.

One day, out of the small allowance my grandfather gave me, I walked to a shoe store and bought her some patent leather slippers. When I gave them to her, she was overjoyed. How happy I felt when she finally had a dress to wear for each day of the week.

Let me emphasize that I did not feel overly magnanimous toward this particular girl. I only knew I longed to introduce both her and others to the God of Love who was my precious Father. For God *had* won me with His Love. It was always present for me, like the love of an earthly father who cared.

AS A YOUNG ADULT . . .

When I was twenty, I felt well enough to take a secretarial job in an engraving and print shop. I can always remember among its line of Christmas cards a special one that would make a lasting impression on me. It showed a little girl dressed in ermine knocking on a big front door. The verse on the card read:

> *I'd like to rap and softly tap*
> *Upon your big front door*
> *Then swing it wide and step inside*
> *And say to you once more*
> MERRY CHRISTMAS!

Curiously, the card never actually said that to me. Rather, the words in my heart were these: Let me knock on *every* door and mend every troubled heart.

At the age of twenty-two, I at long last came to live with my dear mother and my stepfather. My grandfather had died a short time before and my grandmother had given up their old home.

I was happy and working every day at the print shop when one day I suffered an almost fatal heart attack. This attack was so serious that the doctor later told my mother that he was afraid he had been called in to sign the death certificate. A minister was also called in to pray for me.

During this grim bout with death, my grandmother was constantly at my bedside. Once, when I was conscious, I whispered to her a prayer that I would give my life to others if God would let me live. To this my grandmother replied, "When one prays to God so earnestly, I am sure He will answer."

Well, God did answer my prayer. After many months of long struggle, I finally recovered my health. By the time I was twenty-five I had opened my own little gift shop. I felt drawn to this type of business because things of artistic beauty had always captivated me. The shop proved to be a moderate success and I felt tremendously happy in this work.

Then into my shop one day walked a real guardian angel. She was a lovely lady, Dresden-china-like in appearance, and endowed with much God-given talent. She had come to show me a line of decorative items she was selling. I soon found out that she was a skilled artist in her own right.

I immediately fell in love with this woman's work and asked her to make a sign for the door of my new shop. It turned out to be a thing of true beauty, a sort of oval framed vase of flowers with the word "Gifts" on it. I proudly hung it by a silk cord on the front door, knowing it would attract many customers.

This woman, whose name was Hazel Hoffman, and I became staunch friends and I featured her lovely things for as long as I had the shop. Many of the articles she designed and created were like works from Heaven. Someday she was to become a vital part of my own work as the illustrator of my inspirational books.

MARRIAGE AND LATER YEARS . . .

After a few years I gave up the gift shop because the location was being taken over for use as an office building. About this time I married and eventually gave birth to a son, whom I named Val.

My husband was employed by the government as an engineer. At that time he was working on plans for government buildings and later he was with the Post Office Department, designing plans for mail conveyors.

We had a sweet but modest little home. Since I had

done exclusive infant's wear for two large area department stores as well as decorating work, I found it a natural and happy occupation to decorate my own small home. Little by little I furnished it with all white French provincial furniture. I had always liked French things and white seemed so serene and sacred to me.

My dainty, white organdy curtains had ruffles of exquisite embroidery and they were imported handwork. I loved such beautiful handwork for it always made me reflect on the gifts of God expressed through the channel of human lives.

I learned later that the embroidery design on these curtains was called lily of the valley. In the years to come this would hold a special meaning for me because I came to know Jesus Christ as *the* Lily of the Valley in my life and work.

The walls in our small house were of the palest blue. They reminded me of God's heaven painted with the exquisite artistry that only He could create. Under His canopy of blue — which always did something to motivate my thinking — I felt serenity . . . the peace and security of God.

Because I still held a great love for His pink blossoms and the pink colors of my childhood days, this dimension too was woven into my humble decorating scheme. I created little flower bouquets for each room and gorgeous pale pink silk roses for the silver bowl on the dining room table. And I placed baskets of pink silk roses on the floors of the rooms throughout the house.

Very especially a *rose* played a most important part in my decorating scheme. Why this great love for a rose? One day this would be made plain to me by God.

For in the years to come, the ill, the lonely, and the

struggling would come to this tiny house of mine in desperate need of hope. So often they would tell me that they too felt peace in this restful setting. And one day Jesus Christ would also enter my life in this tiny abode. He would be God's one perfect Rose . . . and the joy of all existence to me!

When my little son Val arrived, I told my doctor he was going to be the most wonderful baby in all the world. And to me of course he was. Certainly he was one of the most ribbon-bedecked infants one ever saw for I was reliving my days making infants' ware for the department stores. Val might have been a girl for all of this finery he enjoyed.

As he grew older, Val always remained a happy child. He was also such a comfort to me during the sick days that still plagued my life from time to time. But whatever our problems — and we both had our share — God always helped us through them all.

For example, I recall when Val had the cornea of his eye cut in a freak accident. When a neighbor boy threw a rusty tin can lid across our street, it ricochetted to where my little six-year-old was standing and hit him in the eye.

We rushed Val to the hospital emergency room to see our pediatrician. When he realized the seriousness of the accident, he told us to drive as fast as we could to Washington to consult a special eye surgeon. When Val and I got there, it was way past office hours but this fine man had waited for us. After examining Val's eye, he was uncertain whether to trust nature to do the healing, or subject Val to surgery.

It was ten o'clock before we finally got home that evening — but a decision had been reached. How well I recall that all of us — most importantly the doctor, of course — had

decided to wait and trust to God for the healing, rather than risk the surgery.

The members of the nearby church congregation prayed for Val, including the mother of the boy who had caused the accident. And the boy himself, terribly sorry for what he had done, spent several days reading to Val to cheer him up.

During all of this, I continually felt the love of God reaching out to help my son. I was so happy and relieved when Val was fully recovered, although he had to have intensive eye care for nearly two years. At the end of this time, the surgeon reported that his vision was completely normal again. A few years later, it also gave me pleasure to read in one of Val's school compositions how God and this fine doctor had helped him.

Despite these adversities in my life, my ever-present God balanced such things with happier things. I remember being room mother several times at Val's school. I wanted to be as active as I could there and so I planned treats and dainty things for the young peoples' parties from behind the scenes. Often Val would say, "Mom, please take that job again — you give us better things for our parties than the other mothers."

I remember too how I would tell Val good-night from his little room that faced the small church chapel diagonally across the street from our house. At this time the big church itself was being completed, and the day finally came when I saw the huge crane being used to attach the steeple. When at last the finished steeple stood straight and tall on the new church, it brought to mind these words that would later be recorded in one of my books:

As it had been during my childhood days, Christmas was always a special day for Val and me. I collected dolls for the poor one year, and as a teenager Val would put on a red Santa Claus suit and collect toys for them, too. Then he and his friends would gather in our recreation room, tie up the presents with fancy paper and ribbons, and deliver them. Val would return and enthusiastically tell me how much of a joy it was to do this. To him it was the sweetest part of Christmas to hold a poor child on his knee.

Every Christmas Val would get his friends to sing carols on the corner near our house. Before this he would lavishly trim the front of the house and the lamp post with lights and ornaments. And I would find such joy in creating a most beautiful wreath for our door. Added to this would be the hymns of Christmas pealing joyously forth from the big church across the street.

Then came the day to send Val off to college. I recall with what excitement we had looked forward to that day. Yet when it finally came, both of us were strangely sad, for we sensed how much we would miss each other.

But God had a plan to unfold in my life — a plan that I had never dreamed of. Soon it was to give my life its greatest meaning! At last that long-ago promise — to give my life to others if God would let me live — would become a holy mandate to help others through the power and blessing of God.

My Mission begins ...I am Touched by The Master

With my son Val now off to college, and of course my husband busy at work, I spent many hours alone, except for the company of our faithful maid, Dotsie Proctor. My heart specialist had placed me on a heart rest-cure program, which created some loneliness and much time to think.

As these shut-in days went by, many troubled hearts came to my room to cheer me up, but they ended by pouring out their own troubles to me. Sharing many such hours with these people made me long to find a way to bring them to Jesus and His hope.

I begged God to use my life to help them. Naturally, I had no idea what course He would take. I had never aspired to writing before and had had no formal theological background. Even so, God took over and I became part of a far-reaching mission of love . . . for at long last I came to know the matchless Jesus.

During this shut-in period, with so much time to ponder life through, that old promise I had made to God at age twenty-two — after my near-fatal heart illness — kept gnawing at my conscience. And as I thought about these troubled lives that came to my room, another thought also filled my days: "Where is that still small voice that shall come out of nowhere to tell them God is Love?" In other words, I was constantly longing to fulfill this mission of bringing God into the lives of others because He Himself had given me so much love ever since my insecure girlhood.

Well, God must have understood that longing because one glorious day in 1958 a stranger came to our house to do business with my husband. He soon became a friend of the family and thereafter came to see us often. Once he brought me a small volume of the New Testament, telling me it had been issued him in the service. He added: "I am ashamed to tell you, but this has been in one of my drawers for ten years ..." Then he went on to say: "I somehow feel you have a sweet association with God and I would rather give the Book to you than anyone else in the world."

Next my friend took a white carnation from the lapel of his coat, which he had worn as he ushered at church, handed it to me, and I felt a mission had begun. I continued to wonder what this man saw in me that made him feel that I had a "sweet association" with God. Why had he given me the tiny New Testament? I would soon find out in the days ahead.

When troubled people with whom I visited and tried to help left my room, I found myself searching hours on end in this tiny Testament for the promises of God's love most pertinent to each of their individual needs. What did Jesus

actually say when this one needed inspiration, that one faith, or another hope? As I searched for these wise words — and found them — the Bible became for me a beautiful love story. Before my eyes was a language of love that all hearts were seeking. I then realized that when every theologian had expressed his last view and when every author had penned his best work, Christ had still summed it all up perfectly in three short words: God Is Love!

Yes, God's love was indeed the answer, the secret of it all. Through Jesus's divine ministry I came to know that the promises of God were guaranteed. We only encountered defeat when we doubted those words. For the Bible could never be reduced to a scientific instrument; if it were, it would surely lose its beautiful meaning and its truth. For the Bible consisted of a single theme of love — a simple matter of loving and believing!

And further, the things we could not quite grasp or understand, Christ taught us to trust to God for. In so doing, our faith would be strengthened. As the Scripture points out in Romans 8:24: ". . . hope that is seen is not hope; for what a man seeth, why doth he yet hope for?"

Suddenly, too, I could see that my own life was changing — and changing for the better. I felt less ill each day and became caught up in a spiritual glow of happiness such as I had never experienced before. At long last I had come to know Jesus Himself — not just things about Him.

These days became truly wonderful and I felt like saying to all who came to see me: "Yes, I have met the Master and have been touched by His love!" Hope had indeed become mine and I had enough to share with all.

Sometimes, when I thought of my own interrupted schooling, I was amazed that God had sent me the greatest Teacher of all to guide me each step of the way. As His beautiful promises unfolded concerning matters of faith, hope, and love, I often looked up to my God and said aloud: "Everything is answered . . . Jesus has left us the Word."

Fortified with these reassuring promises, I often sat on the side of my bed and begged God to use my life to help the ill, the destitute, and the struggling. I implored Him to go with me along the highways and by-ways of life, to the lonely farm houses, the bleak hospital rooms, and to take them words of love. Once I was moved to write:

I am grateful for these
loving promises to lean on:
In Him nothing is hopeless . . .
And He is always near.
Beams of light from the halo of
    his loving head
Shall illuminate our path to Hope.

In the days to follow — it was now the happy year of 1960 — I worked with the ill, the lonely, and the struggling who called me on the telephone or visited me. I offered them these promises of Jesus Christ combined with my own humble thoughts. I began to find my own heart filled with affectionate sentiments and with little original prayers and verses. I felt within me the sudden and compelling urge to write. In this way, perhaps, I might be able to reach and help more people.

And before I knew it, God had helped me to actually

create some small pages of manuscript which were to become my very first book. Its title would be *The Greatest of These Is Love*.

In God's divine plan, this little book would have a sympathetic page for each human need, offering the reassuring promises of Christ combined with my own humble thoughts. There would be a page for hope, faith, love, as well as a page for those who were weary, bereaved, and subject to other human vulnerabilities. As I worked on the page about love, spontaneous thoughts like the following would occur to me and I would quickly write them down:

> *Who created a flower to bloom*
> *Who designed a prayer*
> *Who dreamed up the joy of love?*
> *— Only the God we share.*

All the while I knew this sacred thinking welling up within me was God-inspired — not thoughts of my own but created by God and God alone. It seemed that God was grooming me to do His mission and that He might even let me be the channel through which His words could flow. Under this divine inspiration and motivation, I grew to thinking about how those who gave the accounts as recorded in the Holy Bible must have felt. It all confirmed in my heart that the Bible was the final and irrevocable word of God. There was no need to question its authenticity, to doubt, but instead to accept with our minds the things we could comprehend and leave the rest up to God in complete faith.

If ever my life had known celestial moments it was in

the year 1960. I will never forget going into my living room with hands folded in prayer, then looking up to God and saying:

Father, take my hand in Thine
Let me serve through love Divine
If some heart should lose its way
Let me be the one to pray
Like a candle shed the light
Till Thy Presence is in sight.

Even as I relate this, I am filled with tears of joy for I shall never forget that experience when I felt that God actually reached down from heaven and *took my hand*. At that precise moment, I thanked God with all my heart for the gift of His Son . . . this Saviour of perfect love.

I had never known such a fulfilling Companion in my life before and, in this unique association with Jesus, I was certain that great changes were to be wrought in my life from then on. Yes, I had been *touched by the Master*. I was sure of it.

This was precisely when I knew that I could no longer settle for less than the perfection I saw in Him. I tended to forget the insecure childhood I had had, and the strain of the various illnesses I had suffered. Rather, I enjoyed the days ahead for what they were — filled with hope and faith. Indeed, as I had been touched by the Master, so I was touched by His love!

Meditating on the divine forgiveness exhibited in Jesus's ministry, I could not help but remember that He was the one perfect love with the right to condemn souls, but was always willing to forgive us our human frailties and grant us a new start if we should ask it.

Doubtless one of the most touching moments in Christ's whole life — to me at least — was when one of the two thieves being crucified with Christ admitted to the other thief that they were guilty, but that this man — meaning Christ — had done no wrong. The same thief then said to Jesus: "Remember me, Lord . . . ." And Jesus answered him, saying, " . . . . This day thou shalt be with me in paradise."

When I realized how quickly and unselfishly Christ forgave this hardened criminal and drew him unto Himself in paradise, I thought: How certainly He will befriend each of His children in their hour of need. So meditating, I wrote these words reflecting the forgiving qualities of Christ's nature:

Father forgive, they know not
what they do
That thou didst send Me
To teach the way to You
In sweet compassion
For them I pray
Trust them, believe them
Keep them this day
Strengthen their faith in
my love so true
Father forgive them, they
know not what they do

Father forgive, they know not
what they do
That I was pleading
To bring them to You
In tender passion
Again I pray
Guide them, please Father
Love them this day
Inspire their hearts to
serve Thee anew
Father forgive them, they
know not what they do.

What a fruitful association I had with Jesus day in and day out as I continued to write my inspirational verses. The manuscript was growing and I wondered at this new gift that God had given me. While I wrote, I slowly came to understand that God had created life like a beautiful garden and that the only true way to Him was by walking in His footsteps in that sacred garden.

Thus, in the days ahead, I met often with Jesus in this garden of life. There I could walk and talk with Him and He would always understand. So satisfying were these moments that I recorded them as follows in *The Greatest of These Is Love:*

> *He will take us in the Garden*
> *We will kneel and He will pardon*
> *As we pause beside Him praying*
> *We will hear our Master saying*
> *Give your hearts to Me this day*
> *In the Garden we will stay.*
>
> *Midst the sunshine and the flowers*
> *Life will seem like heavenly bowers*
> *And our hearts will turn to singing*
> *And our souls with joy be ringing*
> *As we sigh and dream and pray*
> *On that gorgeous sacred way.*

> *We will put our arms around Him*
> *We will kneel because we've found Him*
> *With our love we will caress Him*
> *With our hearts we will possess Him*
> *And we'll walk there every day*
> *With our Saviour just to pray.*

As the current phrase goes, Jesus had "told it like it was" when He said: "...heaven and earth shall pass away but My words shall never pass away." And the farther I progressed with my verses, the more they became rooted in Christ's promises as He offered them in His ministry.

I now spent my days not only typing and retyping these little verses, but I would also try them out on my ill and lonely friends who came to my home or talked with me on the phone. As I attempted to help these people, I realized that God would always have time for us, no matter what our mistakes or needs. He would still forgive us and bless us if we turned to Him. So thinking, I wrote:

We have never gone to Him
and found Him not there
His love has always been
consistently the same
As strong at the eventide
as it was at the dawning
We will never go to Him
and find Him not there
We will never seek Him
trying to do better
and He not hear
And we will never do better
and not find that He
rewards us.

35

So I came to understand that true happiness was a gift of God's grace. God had created us out of love and secured us in the love of a wonderful Saviour. For He was, purely and simply, a Saviour who would lay down His life for His friends.

I myself was not spotless or blameless. I had my faults like every other human being. To walk with Jesus was now my goal for I had come to know that when I was not doing my best with life, *He* had still been doing the best *for me*.

One day I took a little two-inch picture I had of Jesus praying in Gethsemane and painted a tiny gold edge around it. Then I fastened it to the wall in my dressing closet and underneath it I printed these words He had taught me:

> *Therefore I say unto you, What things soever ye desire, when ye pray, believe that ye receive them, and ye shall have them.*

As I studied that dear picture on the closet wall — of Jesus with his hands clasped in prayer — one thought crowded out all others in my heart and soul: that the disciples had not been willing to wait even one hour with Him — in fact, they had fallen asleep — and yet Christ was willing to lay down His precious life for them.

While meditating on His magnificent sacrifice, a ray of light seemed to illuminate that little Gethsemane picture. I hurried and wrote these words concerning Gethsemane which were to appear in my first book:

> *Birds' songs bursting everywhere*
> *Gorgeous flowers perfume the air*
> *Scriptures fulfilled by His prayer*
> *And His love still lingers there*
> *In this place of sweet repose*
> *God gave us a precious ROSE.*

Moved to the uttermost, I told God that I would come here each day and meet with the Master in prayer for others. I promised Him that this little closet would become a chapel to please Him.

And, indeed, I can say today that by the miracle of God it has become a Chapel of Answered Prayer. In bringing the needs of the less fortunate to this quiet little place, my own faith is strengthened merely by once again reading the words beneath the picture.

At long last I had completed thirty-nine little pages packed with faith, hope, and love, and I knew that each page represented a beautiful session with Jesus. For that walk with Him had transformed my whole life.

In reverent plea, I asked God to help me do page forty to close these dear promises, thoughts, and verses as tenderly as they had been created in my heart. So I picked up my white Bible and prayerfully opened it. Instantly my eyes fell on these memorable words in Luke (4:20):

"And he closed the book, and he gave it again to the minister . . . ."

I realized at once that here was the perfect ending for my book. It had taken the magnificent talent of God to close the pages of my little manuscript so lovingly. And in the writing of it, I knew that each step of the way had been divinely inspired.

Yes, I knew it was true because I recalled how God had instructed me earlier to introduce the book with these words:

A Gift of favorite passages.
They can answer in perfect
sequence our every need.
HE LEFT US THE WORD . . .
We have only to inquire of
these loving Scriptures.

It was now early in 1961 and the manuscript was finished. I then turned it over to my dear friend, Hazel Hoffman, the lovely artist of my gift shop days. I asked her to illustrate the pages of it as movingly and vividly as she could. Hazel took the manuscript and promised to do her best. In a short time, she more than surpassed my expectations by creating truly lovely pictures for the book. Each page was framed with pastel floral motifs of roses, lilies of the valley, and forget-me-nots. Roses were used in profusion reflecting Jesus Christ as the one perfect Rose of all existence.

I then secured the name of a publisher in New England, a prestigious company well known for its publications in the field of faith and inspiration. I wrote a letter to the president of this fine company, simply saying: "Will you take my hand in a mission of love? It could be one of the most rewarding missions of your entire life."

In time, this publisher, Mr. Robert G. Bowman, whom I have come to know and respect as a wonderful man, granted me permission to submit my manuscript.

I shall always remember how the pages of the manuscript were bound together with pink velvet. And the illustrations looked like something only the Lord Himself could have bestowed. And I had wrapped up the whole package in such an elaborate fashion that Mr. Bowman, as he later confessed, declared that it looked like a birthday cake when it reached his desk.

But before I wrapped up and sent off the book, I had asked my beloved minister, Dr. James L. Robertson, to come for a moment or two to my home and say a prayer for its success. (I must say that I had already lifted up the little manuscript to God myself in my tiny closet chapel — for His blessing.) Dr. Robertson graciously consented and when he arrived he took me in his arms, both of us standing in the middle of my living room, and prayed to God that my humble work would be accepted by Mr. Bowman for publication.

Not too long after this, on one memorable day in July of 1961, I was in my little closet chapel praying to God for the manuscript's acceptance, when I heard the postman's truck out front. I wondered what he had brought and hurried to the door, thinking to myself, "Well, there's probably no word again today." But I was so wrong! The postman had placed at my door a letter from Mr. Bowman's publishing company, informing me: "We will do the book."

There will never be words adequate enough to express my joy at that moment, and how I thanked God with all my heart. Simultaneously, I knew that He had granted me an inspired instrument with which to reach more and more people who needed comfort through His word.

As I awaited the actual publication of the book, I worked harder than ever with the ill and the troubled people who needed God's help. They came to me from all directions in God's master plan. And, in being able to do something for them, I witnessed the promises of Jesus Christ confirmed and fulfilled as never before.

Two months after the manuscript had been accepted, I again fell ill and my only sister underwent serious surgery during the same month, September 1961. In spite of these setbacks, I was now fortified with the hope of Jesus Christ, for it was to Him that I turned for help in my adversity. Thus, leaning on Him with all my heart and mind, I saw my sister gradually recover from her illness — and in due time I myself was able to work again.

Yet I remember that before I fully recovered, my illness took a turn for the worse — so much so that my doctor became extremely concerned about me. One Sunday morning, so weak that I could hardly pray, I watched my nurse turn on the television set at the foot of my bed. The channel happened to be the one on which Oral Roberts was preaching a sermon. In later years, I came to know this distinguished man of God personally and he has been kind enough to take an interest in my work.

That morning Oral was saying that whatever our needs or burdens, we should attempt to make an immediate and direct contact with God and we would be helped. He said, "Grab a chair, a table, or anything nearby . . . just to be sure you make a direct contact with God."

In my heart I knew that we did not literally have to grab any material thing, but in sheer excitement and renewed hope through listening to Oral's inspiring words, I did reach out and feebly touched the white night table by my bed. Almost instantly I felt the soothing love of God flowing into my body. I am certain it was instrumental in speeding my recovery.

As soon as I could, I went on with my dedicated work more diligently than ever. Day after day I saw Jesus mending broken hearts and helping tragic lives. I saw Him healing the sick and granting new hope. What worthwhile days and hours to spend as I awaited the release of my first little book, *The Greatest of These Is Love!*

Under this spell of His love, I renewed my promise to give my all to God for the abundant help he had given me

and, indeed, all humanity.

Now, since my life had been touched by the Master in so many ways, I felt it only fair that I make this declaration to Him:

> *Yes, I have been there, ever since we met, Precious Master. What you have suffered is my concern — that my life may exist to reflect your perfection on earth and that I may go forth and preach the gospel to every living creature as you so lovingly bade me do.*

> *Yes, my loving Saviour, I was there, and it is the total aim of my heart and soul to be beside You in word and deed all the days of my life.*

> *Thanks be to God, dear Jesus, a rose-scented fragrance lingers at the cross, reflecting your sacrifice, your forgiveness, and your eternal hope!*

Then came that thrilling moment in 1962 when the postman arrived with a copy of my first published book. It was a Saturday morning, the sunshine was streaming into my room, and as I first leafed through the book I relived those moments with Jesus and a flood of gratitude filled me.

The book itself was a dream creation if I had ever seen one. It had a lovely white cover and garlands of roses framed the title which was printed in gold lettering. The text was printed in soft blue and each page was framed with dainty flowers. And the publishers had packaged it in a beautiful gift box. So, by the generous will of God, my little book had become a reality. Truly, it was a gift of love from the Father Himself.

Then I really knew, beyond the shadow of a doubt, that "man has not works to boast of . . . all things are possible only in God." All this happiness had been granted in answer to my prayer.

Yet I couldn't help recalling — in that moment of success — all those months I had spent as a shut-in. During that time, while I was working on that first book — and in the months after its publication — my life literally became a mission for the sick, the isolated, and the burdened. My telephone became a direct line to the troubled. People seemed to contact me from everywhere with their heavy hearts. And, especially in the months following the publication of *The Greatest of These Is Love,* mail poured in to my home.

I'd like to recall a few of these cases now, for in whatever way I was able to help them, I know it was all a part of God's Divine Plan.

I remember one man who had read my book called me one day, and we became friends. Then, during one of our conversations, he admitted to me, almost casually: "Do you know? Just before I met you, I was going to use a gun on myself. I was going to commit suicide. But then I happened to come across a copy of your book, and now I live by page 15 of it."

That particular page ends with these words:

God knows our needs before we make our supplications, and when we receive His answers they are more wonderful than we would have known to ask for.

Then there was the father whose young son was nearly electrocuted in an unfortunate electrical accident. For weeks the boy was unconscious most of the time and his life hung in the balance. In spite of all an entire staff of doctors could do, there was considerable doubt about whether the boy would live.

Distraught, the father turned to me, and I implored God to help me bring this man hope. Soon God gave me the idea of how I could do it. I typed some of the promises of God's love for this man's particular need on a sheet of paper and asked him to carry them with him at all times. I told him to read them once in a while and never once to doubt God.

This father did as I wished and began to lean on God with absolute faith. Each time he called me, he repeated these words: "My son will live . . . I will never give up on God."

And this is exactly what happened. The boy recovered. I was so happy one day when I saw them both in the street together. The father was encouraging the boy to walk and the two of them were laughing every step of the way.

I shall never forget the letter that came to me from Bangalore, India. It was from a student who was studying literature and he said that my book had been recommended to him by his professor.

From his letter, I could see that this young man was

angry, even resentful. He asked me why I believed in God, saying that he himself was an atheist. He also inquired why it should be that God — if there were one — had given me some success as an author while he remained a poor struggling writer.

This letter was a real challenge to me for I wanted desperately to introduce this young life to Jesus Christ. So I went into the little dressing closet in my bedroom, where I have the picture of Christ praying in the Garden of Gethsemane, and read again the words I had written underneath it. Then I asked God to help me bring this young man's life to Him.

My heart thus fortified with new hope, I wrote to the youth in far away India, telling him with all my heart why I believed in Him. I mailed the letter with a prayer that Jesus would touch that life.

And soon a never-to-be-forgotten answer came back to me. In large print, he had written: "THANK GOD FOR YOU, AUDREY McDANIEL, NOW I BELIEVE!" And he added: "Your letter was so sweet; I will help you extend your work of love over here."

And again I knew that another life had been touched by the Master!

One moving case concerned a mother whose son had committed suicide for no apparent reason. The woman somehow blamed herself and isolated herself from her relatives and friends. In her anguish at the loss of her beloved son, she constantly reproved herself with: "Where did I fail him? What did I do wrong?"

Her doctors feared she might do something desperate because nothing they tried seemed to help her. She remained despondent and morose. Eventually the case was brought to me.

I called on the resources of God to help me write a letter of hope that would bring this sad mother into the sunshine of His love once more. I attempted to tell her that she had not failed her son, but that sometimes people like her son feared life itself and that sometimes they acted so hastily in the heat of the moment that no one could be held accountable for their actions.

I further wrote this woman that she must learn to trust God in the shadows as she trusted Him in the sunshine, for sometimes we had to stand alone to prove our spiritual worth to Him. Here, in fact, was her chance to make a contribution to living by not charging these heartbreaks up to God, but instead to so reflect her faith in Him that others might see and do likewise.

That is precisely what this bereaved mother did. She courageously picked up the threads of her life and resumed her once-fruitful place in society. And in my own heart the blessed fact was again confirmed that — in sunshine or shadow — God is there!

Even children sometimes came to me for help.

I remember one night two little boys stopped me in front of my house. One of them said: "We need to see you privately. It's very important." They were neighborhood boys whom I knew and of course I agreed. The smallest, who was about eight, looked up into my face and told me that the day before his mother and father were divorced. His mother had just left the house and was never coming back. The youngster could hardly keep back the tears and his friend had his arm around his shoulders.

I looked into this heartbroken child's face and said: "Darling, there is a wonderful God over you who takes away the problems. So when you go home, try to cheer up your Dad, while your friend here and I try to cheer you up now, and we will make it with God's help. Believe me, it's true."

The boy stared at me for a moment, then said: "Audrey, I cried yesterday, but today I don't think I will have to cry."

I was glad something I had said seemed to help this young victim of a broken marriage, for he walked away with his friend actually smiling.

One night a woman telephoned me and I could hear fear in her voice. She told me she was a clerk in a local store and that she was deeply worried about something. Could she come over and see me? I said of course she could and to come to my home anytime and we would talk things over. She thanked me and abruptly hung up.

Days passed and the woman did not come. Then I got another call from her and, in tears, she told me that she was heartbroken over something she had done. "I kept some money from a sale I made one day," she admitted. "I needed it to buy shoes for a child in my family. I planned to return it as soon as possible. But somebody discovered it and my life's been torture ever since."

That had happened a year ago, the woman said. The store had not discharged her because she'd had a spotless record, but the agony of guilt had been weighing on her mind. She sought forgiveness but did not know how to obtain it.

I hastened to assure her that Christ was a merciful and forgiving Saviour and that, if she truly did repent, the burden would be lifted.

I prayed with her on the phone for several minutes, for the agony this woman was suffering really touched my soul. Then, after my prayers, the woman declared in a voice I knew reflected renewed strength: "Mrs. McDaniel," she said, "this very moment I know this guilt has been lifted from me."

And I, too, knew that it had been. No one could have witnessed more strongly to the power of God to overcome adversity than this new and grateful life!

I witness God's Presence

With the close of 1962 and its successes, I thought the coming months could hardly yield more good things for me. But I was wrong. For one thing, my health had so improved that I was taken off the heart-rest cure. Through the success of my first little book, the work I was doing became better known and a few newspapers had written stories about me. I remember one of them was called "Her Life Is Now a Mission House." In addition, I had been asked to appear on some radio and TV programs and so the mission to which I had dedicated my life received more publicity than I had ever dreamed possible.

That summer I was chosen to give the welcome at the annual conference of the Christian Booksellers Convention in Washington, D.C. And that same year my first radio program came into being. Aired locally on WFAX in Falls Church, Virginia, it was called "Sacred Memory Time." The program consisted of my narrating passages from my book to the accompaniment of moving and inspirational music. "Sacred Memory Time" has been going ever since and has been carried on other stations in many areas of the country. I was also at work on the manuscript for my second book, *Forget-Me-Nots of Love,* for Mr. Bowman. Of course, all these activities brought many more troubled lives to me by way of the mail, telephone calls, and personal visits to my home.

One night my telephone rang and a young man said to me: "Mrs. McDaniel, I could not go to sleep tonight without thanking you for what you have done for me." Surprised, I asked, "Why, what have I done?" The man replied in low, serious tones: "I heard you on my car radio today and I have never heard a more inspiring message in my life."

Then he blurted out: "I was going to take my life. I mean, I was perfectly serious about it. Then I heard you on 'Sacred Memory Time' and your message changed my mind." He went on, "Don't worry about me in the future, though. I'm all right now, thanks to you, and I want to go on being that way."

We chatted quietly for a few more moments, and just before he hung up he said touchingly: "I will pray for you." And as I too replaced the receiver, I thanked God with all my heart that Jesus had managed to touch that life as He had touched mine.

And I remember so well the precious little old lady who was almost blind and who spent her days and hours alone. Two or three times a day she would telephone me and say, "How is the sweetest girl this side of Heaven?" Then she would invariably add: "As long as my heart shall make each successive beat, I shall be listening to your beloved radio program." This went on for many months. Then the phone calls no longer came. I later learned that God had quietly and gently called her home, and that her passing had been painless.

More people now than ever were coming to my little house in search of hope and inspiration. I was moved to write:

Who is your guest? Bring the roses indoors.
Fill thy rooms with happiness. Carpet thy
floor with roses that have been gathered in
word or deed with dear ones. Add thy gra-
ciousness, thy mercy, and thy concern for
all who enter. Encourage a prayer to enter
here.

We ask for God to come to our door
And yet we forget the weary and the poor
When they answer their knock upon our
heart
God is our guest right from the start.

Yes, God was truly our guest, for in every word we uttered and every prayer we offered, *I felt God's Presence.*

Indeed, nowhere did I sometimes feel that Presence more strongly than in the day center whose membership often invited me to be their speaker. I would also show them how to make satin ribbon roses. I cannot forget one elderly couple in my class who were absolutely thrilled at the opportunity to create these little artificial flowers. The husband was a tiny, tottering gentleman who had suffered a very serious heart attack. Yet his uppermost thought in life, it seemed to me, was to be as kind as he could to his nearly blind little wife. He would smile at her, she would smile at him, and then we would all smile at each other. He would say to me as he

squired her around the day center from place to place: "You know, we are so busy taking care of each other." It was so obvious that they were still very much in love.

The tiny sick husband was so eager to learn how to make the satin roses that he would go home, practice hard, and return to the class able to turn out the prettiest roses of anyone. He was so proud of them. Then came the inspiring moment when he finished the best rose he had ever made and pinned it on his little wife — though she could hardly see it. Then he finished another and pinned it on me. Pretty soon, I nicknamed him "Rose Petal Andy."

Not too long afterward, one night in his sleep, Andy went home to God and left his little wife behind. How that little woman grieved for him — that tiny wisp of a man who had sought to care for and protect her. It touched me deeply how she turned to me for comfort and constantly asked her nurse to read my book to her.

Then one day she put her arms around my neck and whispered: "Audrey, I'll be all right — as long as I know *you're there.*" But she was wrong. It wasn't I who mattered. I knew all the while it was God who was really there for her.

At the close of a busy day with the less fortunate, I would kneel to pray. So doing, I would find God Himself there in the dusk of the evening, and once I was moved to write:

Close your eyes and put your heart to rest.
In order that the new day may be more
dedicated to God, ask thyself at daytime's
closing hour, "What have I done for thee
this day?"

As I lay me down to sleep
Heavenly angels guard my keep
God's love the canopy o'er my head
Peace of soul may blanket my bed.

As I tried to humbly minister to the tragically sad and lonely people who sought me out, day after day I saw the Presence of God turn tears into smiles. Thus, I could write in all sincerity in *Forget-Me-Nots of Love*:

> *There is a divine mission in every heart-*
> *break. The disappointments we experience*
> *only tend to turn us to God.*
>
> *These sadnesses are only an interruption of*
> *our happiness that we may come to know*
> *Him, not just about Him, and then we*
> *will never want to leave Him . . .*
>
> *As the cares of life send us to Him, time*
> *and again we learn there is no heartbreak*
> *His love cannot heal.*

51

And I learned just that. For each case that came to me, I saw God take over when we asked in complete faith that He come to the situation. Probably this is why one of the favorite verses in my new book turned out to be this one:

> *Take every dream within your heart*
> *To God who really cares*
> *He longs to hold you in His arms*
> *He listens for your prayers.*
>
> *Take every sigh and every tear*
> *To Him who understands*
> *Exchange these things for lasting peace*
> *Within His loving hands.*

As I waited for this book to be released, I came down with a serious case of pneumonia and had to be cared for by a nurse. But, fortified by hope and faith in Him, I slowly recovered and once more my days were busy trying to help struggling lives. My broadcasts continued to bring mail and callers who needed aid.

I cannot forget the seriously ill woman who, because of her sickness, had to be retired by her company ahead of her normal retirement time. How she dreaded this. Each morning she stopped by my house on her way to work in search of a word of hope. I knew that her illness was getting progressively worse.

Then the day came — and retirement. In distress, she telephoned me and declared that she could not stand being idle all day long. Knowing her many contributions to living, I replied: "Maybe in God's plan you are not retiring at all — but just changing your work."

I remained sad over this woman's plight because she continued to be depressed for days. At length, God moved me to write these words especially for her. I called her and read her the following verse, saying that I intended to use it on my next "Sacred Memory Time" broadcast:

> *God is beside us each step*
> *of the way*
> *If we only lean on His Arm*
> *as we pray*
> *His love is eternal and help*
> *can be wrought*
> *If faith is applied in each*
> *prayer and each thought.*

This pleased her no end and in the days ahead a calming peace came over her life. Then quietly one night, with no

suffering, she passed away. I instinctively knew that she had not "retired" at all. For none of us, in the overall plan of God, ever retire. We simply go on to greater service in a new life. And this woman, my friend, had been transformed through the Saviour's love to more fully express her soul above.

My own life remained as busy as ever. For example, I loved to be invited to be a guest on the program "Talk of Philadelphia," where troubled people could talk directly with me by a special technical hookup. I would leave the program and come home to the Washington area uplifted. Then the mail would pour in and it was so rewarding to learn that something of what we had discussed of God had turned the tide of these lives.

Yes, I seemed to witness God's Presence everywhere.

With His help in 1966, I created a new little book called *Garden of Hope*. From it I should like to share this verse, which turned out to be one of my readers' favorites:

> *If He should pass my way this day*
> *And see me struggling as I pray,*
> *If He should see my soul bowed down*
> *Begging for a peaceful crown*
> *I knew He'd stop along the way*
> *And lift my burden as I pray;*
> *I know that things would be made straight*
> *As if He'd opened Heaven's Gate.*
> *Should clouds again bedim my sky*
> *I'd seek once more this Passer-by*
> *And say again abide with me*
> *For in Thy love is harmony.*

Readers of *this* book should understand, however, that I was not simply creating verses for their own sake. On the contrary, I am certain they were motivated by Him. Indeed, as page after page of *Garden of Hope* was completed, I realized that it was not *I* who created the words, but the Master Himself who inspired them. I was but the instrument through whom they could be put down on paper from the real-life experiences God sent my way.

So it was that I could close *Garden of Hope* with such uplifting words as these:

> *O put thy heart at rest in God*
> *And in His safety dwell*
> *For He alone doth hold thy hand*
> *Thy future can foretell*
> *So lay thee down in peace and sleep*
> *And know that all is well.*

Interspersed with these hours of writing, I witnessed time after time the ways in which the power of God could take over and direct the lives of those troubled people who needed Him.

One wonderful man of my acquaintance, who had lived a truly exemplary life and served his church well, fell critically ill at this time. The illness lingered until it became obvious that it would be fatal. The pain for this friend, in his weakened condition, became more than he could bear. He tried to end it all — and very nearly succeeded. At one point, his heart actually stopped and his chances of recovery seemed zero.

But I remember that by faith and prayer I managed to elevate this man's life into God's protective arms. I was fully convinced that this wonderful man's existence simply could not end on this sad note in God's master plan. And I remain absolutely convinced today that it was through God's infinite power and mercy that this man recovered and lived on for many years to serve the less fortunate.

All the while during these cases my heart was overjoyed for God had given me the only job I ever wanted in life: to keep that promise to give my life to others if He would let me live. I knew that I had no healing power of my own, of course, nor any ability to move mountains, save to ask God through unshakable faith to help these dear lives. And my loving God always understood and gave His perfect answer.

I remember another elderly man — one who had led a kindly, generous life and who delighted in helping the poor — who could not quite understand the teachings of the Bible nor could he bring himself to accept Jesus Christ. He questioned how God could sacrifice His Son on the cross if He was a God of love.

I talked with this fine man time and again, trying to explain the beautiful way of God to him. And in the months that followed our talks, I prayed to God to help this person accept His Son, Jesus Christ.

Then one beautiful Easter Sunday morning I attended church. It all seemed so divine, with the lilies on the altar and the lovely Easter message of hope. After church, I somehow felt moved to visit this elderly man. I found him ill in bed. And, to my total surprise, he said to me: "Audrey, pray for me, for I now accept Jesus Christ!"

I have never lived a more rewarding Easter Sunday in my life. I recall that I placed my hands on this dear man's head and prayed to God with thanks, for another life had been drawn to Jesus Christ. That man lived on to be ninety before he went home to God. But I will never forget those inspiring moments we shared together when his life — like my own — was touched by the Master.

In 1967 another miracle was granted in my work. It came about in a wonderful way in God's plan. My sister, Dorothy, who has played the piano beautifully by ear ever since four years of age, told me one day that the verses from my books were constantly going around in her head, even in the wee hours of the night. Then she found herself creating a melody for my little prayer "His Presence" — the prayer I had made to God to let me serve Him through His love, which opens with the line "Father, take my hand in Thine" and is quoted in full earlier in this book.

We both became quite excited by this and so we called in a music arranger. He took down the notes for this fledgling hymn just as Dorothy played the notes on the piano. Hearing about this new music, Harold Flammer, Inc., the well known choral music publisher, immediately published it. This same hymn went on to become the theme music for my inspirational programs on radio and TV. It was also later recorded by The Living Strings in their album "Songs of Inspiration."

Harold Flammer, Inc. then asked Dorothy and me to create a hymn book which would include this hymn and eleven more. This we were delighted to do and it was called "Hymn Gems from Sacred Memory Time." Dorothy composed the music and I contributed the words.

Thus God continued to bless me and, in all I did and thought and said, I continued to witness His Presence everywhere.

The burdened and ill still came my way, of course, and I recall the tiny deaf lady who was so heavy-hearted. She sat with me over a cup of tea in my home one day and poured out her troubles. I could see she was almost at the breaking point and she begged me to pray for her. Her little grandson, who was seriously ill, was scheduled for surgery on Monday. She added that her life was so burdened in so many ways that she might herself be to blame for her grandson's condition. This was only Saturday and the thought of waiting for the outcome of Monday's surgery was too distressful. What she was asking was: How can I come to God?

Here was a question so often asked of me in the past that I had included a short treatment of it in one of my books. I went and got the book and read her this part. In fact, I told her to take the book home and read it completely through. When she left, I thought she looked a bit brighter.

Just two days later, on Sunday, she called with a joyous note in her voice: "Audrey, miracles have been happening in my life! Really! Most important, the doctors say my little grandson won't have to have surgery after all, and that he'll be all right. And since I saw you, I've been asked to help in some religious activities that I've wanted to take part in for some time. Finally, I've been reading your book over and over and the ideas in it are really changing my life!"

This woman's life became the happiest I believe I have ever known in the work I was trying to do. I knew it was not actually my book so much that changed her life, but the promises of Christ in it that had brought her happiness and peace. Indeed, all credit belongs to Him. I only prayed for the privilege of serving in His plan.

About this time I became acquainted with a young man who had been accidentally shot and was paralyzed from the shoulders down. He could, however, manage to type with one partially-closed hand, lying down. A brilliant person, he was so eager to become a professional writer. Yet, understandably, he often became discouraged and would telephone me to tell me his script was not going the way he wanted it to.

I would try to encourage him by saying, "Look, when you have finished each line, think of my being right beside you, praying for you and believing in you. I *know* you can do it!" This would send him back to his typewriter with renewed enthusiasm and soon he might call me back and read a revised script that pleased him.

After praying earnestly for his success, I wrote to some editors I knew, told them about this young man's handicap, and asked if he might submit some of his material to them. They said they'd be happy to see it. While he got his share of rejection slips, it wasn't long before he began selling a few articles. This gave him the confidence he needed, and soon he was asked to do a radio script and shortly after that his own column.

As he went on to more successes, I knew that the changes wrought in his life were due to a loving God who had answered a prayer of faith. My small part in the case mattered little for He had heard and responded according to God's Divine Plan.

The year 1969 brought many good things my way, including my newest book, *God Is There*. In beginning to write this book, I remembered something my son Val had said to me when he was a teenager: "Mother, religion means to me the way you speak of love. When I see a rose, or breathe God's fresh air, I know that God is there!" This had motivated me to open the book with this thought:

> *In the heart of a rose ...*
> *in fragrant air ... in*
> *sunshine or shadow ...*
> *GOD IS THERE.*

How well, too, I remembered the constructive prayer sessions with the tragically burdened during those months. So I was inspired to write in this book:

In the presence of the Master
Communing with Him there
I will place your name before Him
In my silent, sacred prayer.

I had come to have many such thoughts as these as I tried to lift up the spirits of those who came to me for help. In particular, I can never forget one dear lady who had suffered much illness in her life and had had to have surgery many times. One day she came to my home in excruciating pain and begged me to pray that her pain be taken away. This pain was due to ear trouble she had developed and there was much draining. In desperation, she had consulted three doctors and taken the medicine they prescribed, but still the pain would not go away. Of course, I prayed for her, but the pain persisted.

A couple of nights later she telephoned me and begged again for some sort of prayer that would relieve the terrible pain. I knew now that I must somehow summon up the most powerful kind of prayer that I could muster. So I turned directly to God Himself and said aloud while we were on the phone: "I know in absolute faith that Jesus is willing and able to help this struggling loved one. I know that You are a God of Love and it is Your pleasure to take care of Your own. Yet I implore You to take care of this soul *now!*"

Suddenly I felt the peace of God in my heart. At the same moment there flashed into my mind the Biblical account of

Jesus healing the blind man and how the scales fell from that man's eyes. Magically too I somehow felt that, even as I spoke to this pained woman over the phone, the "scales" had dropped from her ears. And, in actual fact, I learned in the following days that this terribly painful ear trouble of hers had miraculously cleared up — without medication.

It was certainly not I, but God, who had moved that mountain. For I knew on the phone that day that God was helping her and I knew that Jesus was willing and able to give her aid through the Holy Spirit working through me.

Little did I know that my own faith was soon to be tested, and that I might have written the following verse from *God Is There* for myself:

> *O take God's hand*
>   *He's calling you*
> *He offers help*
>   *in all you do*
> *Let not life's cares*
>   *your heart dismay*
> *God's planned for you*
>   *a better way.*
>
> *Then turn from fear*
>   *let faith abide*
> *Your gracious Lord*
>   *is on your side*
> *Kneel down in peace*
>   *and gently pray*
> *For Jesus said . . .*
>   *I AM THE WAY.*

That year my husband became critically ill. The doctors diagnosed his condition as cancer of the lung which had to be removed immediately. Here were moments of real stress that I had to live through, for the doctors could offer me little hope that he would recover. But I managed to hang on to God and, as I prayed, I saw help coming through. Even the doctors were surprised when he survived the very serious surgery involved and slowly recovered his health.

That is why the following passages from a page in *God Is There* have such special meaning for me now:

> *Lift up your heart . . . In God there will always be hope!*

> *We are His very own and He really and truly takes care of us when shadows overtake us.*

> *Life was not made for sorrow . . . and His dear, precious love can give . . . a sweeter tomorrow.*

At this point I would like to share with my readers something very unusual that happened to me one day. I know that some people will smile and say that I was surely imagining things, but I cannot help that. To me, nothing could have been more real on this earth.

It was a late Sunday afternoon and I was all dressed up because Val was having some of his young friends in. One minute the house was ringing with their happy laughter, the next they had suddenly all left and the house was absolutely quiet and rather lonely.

I went into my living room and looked up to God and said: "Father, I wish I could go out all dressed up in this pretty dress!" No sooner were the words out of my mouth than I realized how foolish and selfish they sounded. Then I told God: "I'm sorry I said that to You. I'd much rather be dressed up in a pretty way of heart and soul for You than anyone else in the world." In His infinite wisdom, I think God had known that I just longed to go out and have a little fun for I was still somewhat of a shut-in.

The next thing I knew I had an intensely powerful feeling that Jesus was standing outside my door, knocking to come in. And I said in my heart to Him, "O, please come in, Saviour. Master, do come in."

And in the excitement of it all, without really stopping to think what I was doing, I hurried to the kitchen, grabbed two lace place mats, and filled two cups with tea. I set a place for Jesus and one for me. I did not actually see Jesus, nor did I audibly hear Him, but the fact that His Presence was there and that he had come to sup with me I never doubted for a single moment.

I drank my tea with a glowingly happy feeling inside me. When I looked over to His place, I saw the steam still flowing from His cup, and in my heart I distinctly heard Him say: "Now drink from My cup!" And with that, my dear Visitor softly left the room, but the tender memory of His coming to me will never leave my soul.

It was not an imaginary incident. I knew He had come to cheer me. And I had not missed the message He had brought

me. He was offering all of God's blessings for my life — if only I would drink from His cup.

Moreover, this experience made me ponder for days afterward on how long some of us delay in life to ask the Saviour into our hearts — this marvelous Being who first loved us before we ever loved Him!

The sum total of these inspiring experiences caused me to strive even harder to reach more of His children. In the months just ahead I marvel in retrospect at the lives I saw — invariably through prayer to God and reliance on faith in His ways — come out of intensive care for heart attacks, strokes, brain damage, and similar critical illnesses. Further, I witnessed many who had simply lost their way and become separated from God return to His magnanimous fold.

Then personal tragedy struck again. My precious little mother, who was living with my sister Dorothy, suddenly had a stroke. I remember calling the ambulance and riding with her, so critically ill and unconscious, to the hospital. Eventually she recovered sufficiently to be taken to one nursing home and then another. My sister and I would go each day to visit her and we marveled how she quickly regained her former cheery disposition. We marveled, too, at the astonishing number of friends she made at these institutions.

During these long months of my mother's illness, I was working on a new book which was to be published in 1971. It was called *A Christmas Rose* because I considered Jesus the one perfect Rose of all existence. More than that, I knew Christ was God's Christmas Gift of perfect love to all humanity — past, present, and future. I formed the habit of reading to my mother pages of the manuscript and this seemed to cheer her up immensely.

At these times I would recall how Jesus had befriended me during my near-fatal illness years ago and, as that illness finally lifted, it seemed that He said to me: "I have liked sitting here beside you in this illness, but since you are now improving, I guess you will have no further need of me at the moment and I will be going down the road alone." My heart literally rushed after Jesus at that moment and I felt as if I actually touched His white robe. Somehow I could not bear the thought of my beloved Master "going down the road alone." I wanted so for Him to know that I would be there for Him should He want me. Humbly, therefore, I recorded that thought in *A Christmas Rose*:

> *O Jesus how I ponder*
> *Your matchless love for me*
> *And how my Father fashioned*
> *A perfect Gift like Thee*
> *The way you took my burden*
> *And made it all your own*
> *The most unselfish Love of all*
> *The world has ever known*
>
> *You'll not walk that road without me*
> *As if I didn't care*
> *For every time I needed you*
> *I found your dear Heart there*
> *I remember now your faithfulness*
> *Your Love and Comfort too*
> *So let me take your Hand dear Lord*
> *And walk along with You.*

Then, by a miracle of God, another person whom I can truly call a guardian angel came into my life. This was Hayden

Huddleston of Roanoke, Virginia, the well-known radio and TV producer and also head of his own advertising agency. Hayden happened to read my book *A Christmas Rose* when it came off the press. It impressed him so that he telephoned me and said that the book had held him captive and that he "had to do something with it."

I should like at this point to say something about this fine and talented man who later became my good friend. In former years, Hayden had been afflicted with cancer. He had suffered a tumor on the tongue which caused him to have nearly half of his tongue removed. Tragically ill and weak and plagued with an almost total loss of the power of speech, he wondered desperately at the time whether he could find the will and strength to go on living.

Then one day Hayden, shortly after his cancer surgery, was struck with the idea of doing a radio series based on the idea of going to church. It caused him to start thinking more about God and to strengthen his belief in Him. Determined to speak again, Hayden practiced mouthing words into a tape recorder, then turning the volume way up to see whether he was forming words and sentences correctly. By doing this again and again, he found himself able to speak again and, in fact, he went on to become a moving and accomplished broadcaster.

Also, the going-to-church idea stayed in Hayden's mind and soon he found himself writing little one-minute messages to create a series of short programs called "Let's Go to Church." Later the programs were lengthened to five minutes, then eventually to the popular and widely-heard half-hour series that it is today.

At any rate, Hayden was so taken with my little Christmas book that he produced a brilliant thirty-minute special for TV and radio titled "A Christmas Rose." He himself would do the narrating and it was scheduled to be broadcast over many stations on Christmas Eve, December 24, 1971.

Excitedly, I kept telling my beloved mother, "Mom, I will

have to try to get you out of bed and into the wheelchair so you can go to the TV room of the hospital. Then you can watch our wonderful Special on Christmas Eve."

Well, Mom didn't quite make it. On December 23, the night before Christmas Eve, she was called home to God. But when the special went on the air, I knew Mom was now whole once more, without pain, and in the sheltering arms of God where the afflictions of this life could no longer touch her. What's more, I was sure that she was watching our Christmas Special about the Master.

During the coming year, I became involved even more deeply in inspirational work and writing. I also kept hearing all kinds of things about the workings of the Holy Spirit in peoples' lives. These stories puzzled me for I had never experienced such a phenomenon in my own life.

I had heard some people say, for example, that instant cures for their ills had taken place. They had related how warm feelings had gone through their physical bodies, sometimes so powerful that they had been struck to the floor by them. There were all kinds of testimonies which set me to pondering.

Eventually I simply told God that I myself had never experienced such things, but that if He wished to reveal them to me, to please will it so.

For up to this time I had only known God and Jesus as tender, patient Love that had come quietly into my life. There had been no emotional or dramatic experiences, yet His love was always totally fulfilling. I had never had any reason to

doubt this Presence; it was confirmed in my heart to the fullest.

Therefore, feeling no distress at not being acquainted with the Holy Spirit as some had related, I moved on in my work, trying to reflect the way of Jesus.

Meanwhile, I came to see as the days passed that Jesus was nothing if not perfect love. I would review His beautiful ministry constantly. Time and again, I realized that of all the things He gave — including faith, hope, confidence, and healing — the greatest of these was still love.

At this same period, I was also spiritually moved by His prayer in the beautiful passage of John 17:9 beginning: "I pray for them . . . ." It was these words that inspired me to write: in my early book, *The Greatest of These Is Love:*

> *Here Jesus is sponsoring us before God in His final hour; not praying for His own concern, but beseeching God to have faith in us.* NOTHING *will ever reach the heights of devotion found in "I pray for them."*

Here one is inspired to think of a Saviour facing a cruel cross, despised, rejected, and condemned, yet still sponsoring us before His God. O! His unselfish concern for those He loved!

It is also uplifting to contemplate how He still tried to fortify the ones He loved as He talked with the disciples, as set forth in the beautiful passages in John 16:26-27. There again, due to face a cruel cross, he nevertheless tried to comfort those He loved as He left them. In short, Jesus was thinking not of Himself but always of us.

So, I continued to ponder what else on earth Jesus could have offered us in His divine ministry. What greater comfort could He have possibly given us?

And then one glorious day — not by chance, I am sure, but through divine will — my eyes fell upon the Scriptures in John 14:16 and John 14:26. This was the moment when I was introduced to the beautiful Holy Spirit.

Here again, Jesus was realizing that He was soon to depart from those He loved, yet with His compassionate heart He still thought of their welfare, not His own. Thus His prayer in John 14:16: "And I will pray the Father, and he shall give you another Comforter, that he may abide with you for ever."

And in the magnificent Verse 26, Jesus said: "But the Comforter, which is the Holy Ghost, whom the Father will send in my name, he shall teach you all things, and bring all things to your remembrance, whatsoever I have said unto you."

Finally, in the unforgettable Verse 27, Jesus offers His peace: "....Let not your heart be troubled, neither let it be afraid."

Only a divine Saviour like the matchless Jesus could be bringing a sacred ministry to a close with such concern and love for others. In unspeakable happiness, I knew the comforting Holy Spirit was now mine. For Jesus had prayed for this Gift for me and His Father had answered this prayer.

I now fully realized that all of the thoughts for good that motivated my life were the workings of the Holy Spirit in me. The forces that kept me from evil, that preserved my security,

my hope, my faith, my love — all these were really the Holy Spirit bringing to remembrance the things Jesus had taught in His sacred ministry.

Thus it became ever more plain to me that Jesus had established a ministry to the honor and glory of God and that the Holy Spirit had come to magnify that ministry. Yes, I had finally come to comprehend the meaning of a dear Saviour who was perpetually concerned lest we have a sad moment, stumble and fall, lose faith, or despair.

So, like God and Jesus who had entered my life by way of patient and tender love, there had also come the beautiful Holy Spirit. It had come quietly through Scripture. There had been no emotional display, nothing of a dramatic nature, only the restful sensation of simple and fundamental truth flowing over me.

After this experience, I found I could work more fulfillingly with the ill, the lonely, and the struggling. Indeed, I was far better able to help these people because the wondrous Holy Spirit continued to remind me of the promises of God as manifested through the teachings of Jesus Christ.

Truly, in receiving this precious Gift, I had witnessed prayer answered!

That these divine forces were working in my life was evident as my telephone continued to ring with pathetic cases who needed all the help they could get. I remember one dear lady who had first suffered a severe stroke followed by a heart attack. Confined to the intensive care unit in the hospital, she was not expected to live.

In desperation, the woman's husband telephoned me to

say that his wife knew of my work and implored me to pray for her recovery. In fact, the night before she was first taken ill she was gathering together some of the clippings she kept from the column I wrote for a local newspaper; she had planned to send them across the country to places where they would cheer the less fortunate.

With all my heart I talked to God about this dear life, seeking His love and protection for her. A couple of days later, the phone rang and she herself was on the other end of the line, telling me that she was out of intensive care and would soon be sent home. She also told me she was reading my book *Abiding Love* to a woman far sicker than herself, her hospital roommate, who asked that I also pray for her. Which of course I did. Cases like this one often multiplied in such a way, and I was glad to help all that I could.

Another case that touched me deeply involved a woman, a former cancer patient, who had suffered an injured thumb. The nail was gone and the pain was so unbearable that the poor woman could not even let it touch her pillow at night. This naturally resulted in much lost sleep — so much that she could not even count on a normal night's slumber to obtain some relief from the throbbing in her thumb. Despite medical help, the situation had gone on for months.

Appalled at the suffering this poor creature was going through, I implored God as fervently as I knew how to relieve it and give her peace. I knew that complete faith was the answer — for her and for me — that God would bring this about. Well, once more I saw God in action! A short time later, I myself witnessed that thumb almost covered over with a new nail. The swelling had gone, the suffering had ceased.

These were but two of many cases. I also witnessed youngsters in trouble, victims of drug abuse, temporarily involved in court or in jail overnight, and so forth. I not only tried to work with the parents involved, I also talked to the kids themselves and many times I saw God take over and triumph.

I myself knew instinctively that I was only a channel by which God could perform His work. In this sense, I understood that my recent acceptance of the Holy Spirit made it possible to clear that channel to God and keep it open to help others.

And I also saw the Holy Spirit at work in the ever-increasing number of lives who, as never before, were beating a path to my door. I begged God to let me extend my mission to them and to relieve some of the suffering in these struggling lives.

But it seemed that God saw fit to delay this mission a while, for I suffered a serious accident in February of 1972. I had a very nasty fall on the staircase at home and sustained a double fracture of the skull. There was also concussion, a broken right clavicle, and other injuries. I had to be driven to the hospital by the Rescue Squad and there I was put on the critical list. I had to be assigned nurses around the clock.

As soon as I regained consciousness, I told God, Jesus, and the Holy Spirit, too, to hold on tight to me and sustain me, for I wanted so badly to recover and work again. Flowers poured into my room from many people, but for weeks I was allowed no visitors.

Later I was allowed to go home to recover fully but I had to have a nurse for four long months. As I sat helpless and weak in a chair, I beseeched God to make me well enough to go on with my mission.

One Sunday soon thereafter, I received a call from my friend Hayden Huddleston in Roanoke. He told me that he wanted enough of my scripts from my books to produce thirty radio programs for his successful series "Let's Go to Church." He himself was going to narrate them all. I am certain the pleasure this news gave me speeded my eventual recovery.

And so, once again, I witnessed God's Presence in my work and appreciated His dear helping hand when I needed it most.

I realize my Greatest Dream

In the spring of 1973 my book *Abiding Love* appeared. I had now been blessed with several of these little publications, each page of them representing an interlude with the Master. They had all been forged out of real-life experiences and I was deeply moved each time I learned that they had, in some small way, been used to help some struggling life.

In hospitals, particularly, as well as in other places where sickness and sometimes death was present, I was gratified to learn that my humble books were giving pleasure and comfort. I remember one doctor remarking to me that he wished that every person going into surgery could read one of them. Another fine doctor told me that it would do immeasurable good if cases of nervous illness could also read these books. And I was especially touched when I was told that some loved one had gone home to God with one of these little books lying near his or her pillow. And how in some cases a bookmark had been placed in one of them where the person had stopped reading for the last time.

Not that people didn't read them on other occasions. Of course, they did. I knew they had brought happiness to mothers and fathers and others on every conceivable gift occurrence and how sometimes even brides had asked their florists to attach their bridal bouquets to one of my books. Yet I knew that in all this I was but the instrument and the channel for God's work. It was He, and He alone, who had planned things this way.

What I was trying so hard to do in *Abiding Love* was simply to assure humanity that no matter what their individual needs, Jesus would always be beside them with a love capable of abiding forever. For I was convinced that my matchless Jesus had walked the weary cobblestones of His selfless life for one sole purpose: to bring hope to the people of the earth. He was indeed God's one perfect Rose as I wrote:

74

A perfect Rose grew on the earth
In days of long ago
It had a special mission
As you and I both know
It came to earth a tiny Bud
With petals to unfold
That as they opened we might see
Fine jasper and rare gold
Its perfume gave a fragrance rare
Which souls may also do
If we will turn to God above
And to our Lord be true
Then as this Rose had opened wide
Its very heart to see
One knew this was the beauty
God sought in you and me
Then as its blooming ended
In quiet and sweet repose
God planned another mission
For this one precious Rose
That in this world for you and me
One Rose would bloom eternally.

And in *Abiding Love* I tried to convey the beautiful peace of soul that comes with knowing Jesus and trusting in Him:

Dear Father teach me this to know
In stress of life with hope dimmed low
That Thou canst weave a peace supreme
That is so real and not a dream
If in Thy arms we place each care
And understand that Thou art there
Then when our hearts with peace shall flow
To know our Father willed it so
Our anxious hearts to rest in Thee
Thou art our help eternally.

In *Abiding Love* my thoughts, too, were for Mary Magdalene and how she must have felt about Jesus, for she had walked with Him and followed Him ever since He had cast out her burdens. Thus I felt moved to write these lines called "The Love of Easter":

I want to walk with Jesus
  every step of the way
To have His goodness sanctify
  each word I say
To follow Him through valley
To the mountains high above
Down every path, through
  every garden
To offer Him my love
To be like Mary Magdalene
Who walked with Him one day
Who felt such pain and anguish
When they took her Lord away
That Love so real appeared to her
When He her name did say
Then Mary found her peace of soul
When Christ stood there that day
He was her one true love you see
Like Mary may He walk with me.

It had now been some eleven years since the publication of my first book and sometimes I found myself happily reminiscing about all the blessings God had poured out upon me in that time. My writings had received international recognition and my various broadcasts were on many stations around the country. "Sacred Memory Time" especially was still being wonderfully received on radio by my many listeners all over the United States.

In addition, I had prepared the promised scripts for Hayden Huddleston's radio series "Let's Go to Church," and been chosen to be featured on the Channel 4 series in Washington, D.C. called "Faith and Life." The latter is an excellent group of inspirational programs presented by the Council of Churches of Greater Washington, the Jewish community, and the Catholic Archdiocese of Washington. Also, my beautiful Christmas special, "A Christmas Rose," continued to be featured on radio and TV during the holiday season.

Long ago I had determined that part of the proceeds of my books was to go toward the building of Arlington Temple and Community Center, part of our Methodist Church at Rosslyn near my home. I always loved the invitations such as "Come One — Come All" at the center and I was glad to be able in some small way to help with the fund-raising there.

I had been active in committee work, too, and found that I enjoyed it. As a member of The National League of American Pen Women with top honors, I had been a past National Chaplain of that organization. This work meant that I had to attend many elegant affairs which brought me into contact

with all sorts of people — movie stars, radio and TV personalities, recording artists, and sometimes heads of state.

I was sometimes amazed that my humble accomplishments had evidently been sufficient to include me in the *International Who's Who* and similar Who's Who volumes. I had been a guest on many radio and TV talk shows around the country and was always very grateful to their hosts for having me on the air. I was a member of the Poetry Society of London and the International Platform Association made up of talent from twenty-five countries. And, while I had been invited to the White House and diplomatic and social functions around the nation's capital, I think I was always more at home at such functions as sharing Christmas with the poor at the Gospel Mission, where I was sometimes asked to be guest speaker.

All summed up, it was a miracle of love that only God could have performed, for I felt I was the most ordinary of persons. Yet I had no idea at this time just how far my work of love was to be further blessed.

My doctors had taken me off my old rest cure at this time and I was able to get out more and do more. I was writing a column for our *Rosslyn Review* newspaper in Arlington and the response to it was very gratifying. I was able, too, to go to church once more. Attending church was rather special for me, for I did not do so with strict regularity. I have never believed that God forces us to go to church but rather just lovingly invites us.

In the fall of 1973, my mission was still growing and it seemed to me that God had poured out every single blessing He could bestow in helping me to fulfill it. Again I was wrong. For in His divine plan, there was much more to come. I was to *realize my cherished dream.*

It happened this way.

In the summer of 1973 I received an all-important letter from a treasured friend of mine, Marie Smith Schwartz, a noted author, lecturer, and a former White House correspondent for the *Washington Post* during the Eisenhower, Kennedy, Johnson, and Nixon administrations. Marie was now the wife of Arnold Schwartz of New York, a trustee of several universities and colleges in New York State, and is also a vice-president of a large hospital medical center. As these credentials indicate, she is extremely interested in serving God and helping humanity. She had also been a source of great encouragement in my own efforts to help people ever since she wrote a story about my books for the *Post* a number of years ago.

Marie was the instrument through which God directed me into a new phase of my work. In her letter, she suggested that I establish a foundation that could accept contributions from people to help broadcast and disseminate the good news of God's love. Marie pointed out that such contributions would be tax deductible because the foundation would be a non-profit one. Its purpose would be to secure air time for broadcasts of an inspirational nature. Prose and poetry would be narrated with sacred music played in the background and hymns would

be sung by fine soloists. The aim of these broadcasts would be to offer help and hope to the ill, the lonely, the struggling, and the heartbroken. Efforts would also be made to give these people comfort in other ways, such as the printed word.

Marie then proceeded to tell me how to begin to seek an incorporation and then receive a tax-exempt status from the Internal Revenue Service.

As I thought about possibly starting such a foundation, the idea appealed to me more and more. I was thrilled beyond expression at the prospect of broadening my efforts to tell about the love of God to unfortunate people who could profit so from it. After talking it over with my minister, who was enthusiastic about the idea, I took the first steps in the long process of getting a Certificate of Incorporation for The Audrey McDaniel Faith and Hope Foundation.

On October 4, 1973, the State Corporation Commission of Richmond, Virginia granted that incorporation. I shall never forget the kindness of the lovely lady at the Internal Revenue Service who wrote to me so graciously and talked with me long distance about obtaining the tax-exempt status for the Foundation. Upon receiving copies of my books for their files and learning more about what I was trying to do, she commented, "What truly worthwhile work you seem to be doing." Her help was invaluable in getting the papers for the Foundation processed and duly numbered by the IRS in 1974.

The Foundation is described as a non-profit, tax-exempt organization established to strengthen faith and hope by way of the printed word, radio and television, and other means of

communication in the inspirational field. Its goal is to help humanity in all walks of life find hope through faith in God's love, regardless of denomination or creed. The organization is staffed by a team of dedicated volunteer workers, with a Board of Directors also dedicated to this great cause. In addition, a team of non-paid secretaries has been secured to assist me in personally answering the mail of the burdened and prayer requests that are given to me first and then to the Prayer Committee for special attention. I wish I could find adequate words to describe the marvelous help that God has granted in the superb work done by the Prayer Committee.

I think these lines of Scripture from the Gospel of Matthew best express God's promise in the words of Jesus:

And all things, whatsoever ye
shall ask in prayer, believing,
ye shall receive.

Matthew 21:22

An inspiring radio series has been produced by the Foundation called "Abiding Love," which features excerpts from my books narrated by myself to uplifting music. The program has now reached many areas of the country and is bringing a wonderful response by way of letters from people in all walks of life in search of hope.

In appreciation of her loyal counsel, support, and guidance, Marie Schwartz was named an Honorary Director of the Foundation. Many have been the times I have telephoned her

at her home in Connecticut to tell her of the fine responses we were getting to the broadcasts, or when the coffers were low to seek her advice on how we might secure more funds to keep the Foundation's mission on the air.

God had surely blessed me every step of the way in setting up the Foundation. In so doing I came to understand that when God has work for us to do He places the tools in our hands with which to do that work. Yet the mission had not been given to me alone for so many people had helped me.

I remembered how my wonderful brother-in-law and his wife, Dr. and Mrs. W. P. McDaniel of Montana, had provided the money, when I first started out in the sacred work, to buy a typewriter and tape recorder. Then there was my friend, the wonderful and dedicated young man I had met when "Sacred Memory Time" first went on radio station WFAX in 1963. This talented and kind man trained me in broadcasting work. We started at the same time at the station and eventually he became WFAX's General Manager. More recently he has taken on the added responsibility of General Manager and Broadcasting Director of the Foundation.

Nor must I forget to mention my beloved minister, Dr. James L. Robertson, now Vice-President of the Foundation, who had believed in me all the way. This great man of God has done so much to inspire my life, with his sharing heart and dedication to the needs of all he has met on the highway of life. Most importantly, I am in his debt for the dear way in which he presented to me the love of Jesus Christ. I shall forever believe that God provides such guardian angels along the road of life to help us.

Certainly one of these is my friend Mrs. Eugene Henry Rietzke, who is outstanding in the nation's capital for her interest in and contribution to the arts and humanities. She is presently serving as another director of the Foundation. Her lovely son, Renah Blair Rietzke, has now gone home to God, but at a very early age he founded The World Youth Peace Movement. He was one of those rare, inspired young men whose ultimate goal was to bring hope to others. It was my esteemed privilege to dedicate two of my books, *Garden of Hope* and *Abiding Love,* to his dear memory. For his life has left an uplifting effect upon all those who had the distinct honor of knowing him.

Through all of this work I saw the promises of God as manifested through the teachings of Christ work miracles in human lives, just as He had blessed my own life so abundantly. Indeed, I saw proof of His divine will in the fact that my little books, written as they were through the inspiration of the Master, had sold well on the way to two million copies. Not only did letters constantly come in to me revealing the good they had accomplished in God's plan, but portions of them had become the scripts for radio and TV shows and thus had reached millions of listeners and viewers.

Miraculously, it often seemed to me, heads of state, clergymen of many faiths, and distinguished members of the press continued to praise and help extend this work of dedication. And all the while I was awarded the satisfaction of witnessing the healing love of Jesus Christ mend broken hearts,

knit afflicted bodies, and return to His fold those who had
become lost and separated from Him.

And I may say that then — as today — I was moved to
unspeakable joy as I saw prayer answered day in and day out.
For I had always seen clearly that prayer was the way to God
and that faith was the splendid key that would always open
the door.

It was in precisely this way that Jesus had offered a love
of simple truths for all mankind. Not a love of complexity, but
a tender and fundamental love that had its roots in faith and
belief — without a shadow entering in.

As I continued my Foundation work, I constantly saw
the truth of the Bible confirmed. It was clear that we did not
need to know all the answers in accepting its way of love. We
had only to trust God and through that confidence receive His
blessings and perfect answers to our prayers. In other words,
we had to put God in charge of our lives, for try as we might
we could not live them with mere human intelligence. No, it
would forever take God's supreme intelligence to make our
lives right.

Bearing witness to these lives being healed under all kinds
of circumstances, I felt as if I stood at the pool where the
cripple once stood imploring Jesus to heal him. Like that
cripple, I saw my own and other lives increase in faith and
strength by Jesus' willingness and ability to aid them. They
had come to trust Him and one by one I saw them made whole
again.

As for my own mission, I knew that God had heard my

cry to serve. And now this Foundation was being blessed day in and day out by what I could only describe as miraculous accomplishments. The credit alone belonged to God. So deeply did I feel about these things that I vowed to make the following lines my fervent prayer to God:

Dear Lord with every passing day
Teach me to walk Thy sacred way,
And if my brother's path be dim
I'd like to be a light to him,
A candle on the darkest night
To chase the shadows out of sight
That opens up his eyes to see
The beauty of Thy majesty;
And then I'd ask along the way
That Thou would'st teach us how to pray
With open mind and open heart
Till all reveals how great Thou art.

It had now been well over a dozen years since I entered inspirational work and in that time I had learned many valuable lessons. I had come to understand how our burdens build the spiritual muscle of our souls. For it is in the deepest needs of our lives that we seek our closest communion with God. Only then do we come to realize that only as God worketh in us are all things possible:

Our burdens make us
what we are
The shadows are a way
to Him
To show self's lack of
strength and power
That needeth God in every
hour
To teach us as this earth
we trod
All things are possible
in God.

Certainly there was one thing I had come to know and know well. I would never have realized my cherished dream — the Foundation and the blessed work that it permitted me to do — without the precious gift of Christ who had so lovingly touched my life. I had humbly seen that God could use me in such work, and indeed had been grooming me all the while for it. Yes, even during the times when I was not doing the best with my life for Him, He was still doing His best for me.

Yes, I had wandered for a long time in darkness and despair until Jesus came into my life and led the way to God the Father. At first, like Peter, when Christ asked him if he loved Him, I only had the wisdom, as Christ bade Peter, to feed lambs. But as I grew under the guidance and inspiration of God I could at length, as Jesus later bade Peter, graduate to the feeding of sheep. In short, I now believed I had "arrived" in God's eyes — I had attained, with His help, the maturity to do His work as He intended I should. And, of course, the beautiful Holy Spirit — the Spirit of God Himself — was ever motivating me to do even more — to surpass myself.

I believe I can do this in the days to come.

It is all as simple as this: we just have to care enough about serving God and mankind — and God will do the rest. If we say a kind word sometimes to someone who is lonely, share a comforting thought or perform some little task for the ill or burdened we meet along our earthly highway, why it all adds up to God — and we ourselves will feel much better for it and benefit truly by it.

This simple philosophy, I believe, is what was meant when the Scripture refers to a cup of water in His name that shall not return empty-handed, but be multiplied many times and magnified in His grace. This is, I believe, the way to happiness, peace of soul, and life's sweetest fulfillment.

These are, to me, the riches of God's Kingdom on earth as He intended them for us.

And I pray that my Foundation, my work, and my life shall stand forever for the power of God to use human lives for good in the world. To that end I can say reverently and with a heart bursting with gratitude, thanks be to Him for choosing the life of a once-timid and frail little girl for a sacred mission of such ultimate importance.

Finally, I should like to bring a few vital thoughts to readers of this book. Yes, I should like to talk to *you*. Call what I am going to say to you advice, if you will, but I believe there is great potential in your life and that it is based on God-like qualities meant to be expressed *for* God in His own way.

When you least expect it, God can choose you for a sacred mission. Try to learn to recognize the signs when He gives them and do your best to answer His call.

You have no divine power or supreme intelligence of your own, but God can use you as a channel to express his love and wisdom for mankind. You can become a useful servant in God's vineyard — which is the world you live in right now.

Don't be afraid to honor your God and even glorify Him. Whatever your religion, respect and love Him — and that love will be multiplied in your own life.

There is no limit to God's love for you. He is an all-powerful, merciful, and forgiving God. You'll find that if you learn to meet him half-way, there is no end to the love he can send *your* way. Jesus Himself summed it all up in three short words: "God Is Love!"

You can turn to God for help by first turning to Jesus Christ. You can say words like: "Please Saviour, let me walk with You so that I can find my way to God." Or you can make up appropriate words of your own. The important thing is to let Jesus know that you need and seek His help. Sincerely invite Him into your life and He will show you the way to God.

If you are going through some difficult period of your life, you can get the help and strength you need by turning to the Master, Jesus Christ. Through the love He has for you, He will see that you are aided — and you will recognize the aid when it comes.

When you accept Christ into your life, come to trust Him, and count on His help and guidance, you will have feelings of peace and contentment that you have never known before.

You can find happiness by learning to have complete faith in the love Jesus has for you. This faith will help you forget the troubles you have had in the past and help you to solve new problems as they come along. This faith will also help you recognize and feel sorry for the wrong things you may have done in the past and teach you to avoid doing such things in the future.

Try to understand that whatever your needs or wishes are, Jesus is waiting to help you. You have only to open your heart and let Him come in.

Now I shall close this book, for the story has been told of how Jesus Christ helped me keep that long-ago promise to God that if He would let me live I would dedicate my life to others and their welfare. I do so with the prayer below, which is for all of God's children. For just as I was touched by the Master and led by His love, so too can you.

O come to the Garden
And meet Him today
Kneel down by your Saviour
And tenderly pray
There's peace in this haven
There's hope and sweet rest
For Jesus is offering you
All that is best.